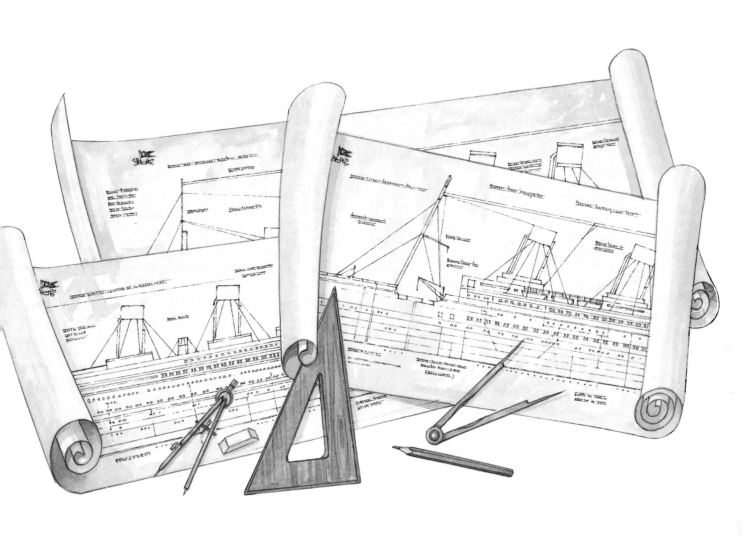

Author:
David Stewart has written many non-fiction books for children, including **You Wouldn't Want to Be an Egyptian Mummy!** He lives in Brighton with his wife and young son.

Artist:
David Antram was born in Brighton, England, in 1958. He studied at Eastbourne College of Art and then worked in advertising for 15 years before becoming a full-time artist. He has illustrated many children's non-fiction books.

Series creator:
David Salariya was born in Dundee, Scotland. He has illustrated a wide range of books and has created and designed many new series for publishers both in the U.K. and overseas. In 1989 he established The Salariya Book Company. He lives in Brighton with his wife, illustrator Shirley Willis, and their son Jonathan.

Editor:
Karen Barker Smith

Created, designed and produced by
The Salariya Book Company Ltd
25 Marlborough Place, Brighton BN1 1 UB

ISBN 0-531-18642-3

12 11 10 9 8 7 6 5 4 3 2 1   1 2 3 4 5

Printed in the U.S.A.

First Scholastic printing, September 2001

You Wouldn't Want to Sail on the Titanic!

One Voyage You'd Rather Not Make

Written by
David Stewart

Illustrated by
David Antram

Created and designed by
David Salariya

SCHOLASTIC INC.

New York Toronto London Auckland Sydney
Mexico City New Delhi Hong Kong Buenos Aires

Contents

Introduction

The year is 1907. Your name is J. Bruce Ismay, and you are the managing director of the White Star Line, a shipping company. Your main rival, Cunard, has just launched the passenger liner *Lusitania*. At 790 feet (241 meters) long, she is huge and very fast. At a London dinner party with William Pirrie, you discuss the highly lucrative sea route between Europe and the United States. Lord Pirrie is a director of Harland and Wolff, the Belfast-based shipbuilders who have built all of White Star's vessels. You decide to think big and plan to build three ships that are heavier than the *Lusitania's* 30,000 tons, and 100 ft (30 m) longer. With luxurious and speedy transatlantic crossings, you will attract the wealthy passenger trade and the growing number of emigrants traveling to North America.

On April 10, 1912, at 12:00, the *Titanic* will leave Southampton, England, on her maiden voyage. The ship will set out to cross the Atlantic Ocean and plans to arrive in New York seven days later. She is the largest ship in the world and, for her wealthy first-class passengers, certainly the most luxurious. At this point, you definitely want to sail on the *Titanic*. Little do you know that the ship is sailing toward disaster...

Designing the Titanic

J. Bruce Ismay

> I have a dream, to build three ships more luxurious than the world has ever seen.

The architects and draftsmen at the Harland and Wolff shipyard work hard to make the planned superliners a reality. While the plans for the ships are drawn up, three dry docks are converted into two — no existing dry dock is large enough to build the huge new liners! On July 29, 1908, the plans are ready. The keel plate for *Olympic*, the first of the three giant liners, is laid on December 16, 1908. The keel plate for the second liner is laid three months later, on March 31, 1909. Her name is *Titanic*.

You were born in Liverpool, England, in 1862. Your father founded the White Star Shipping Line in 1869. In 1902, the White Star Line was sold to American financier J.P. Morgan, but you stayed on as managing director.

Although *Olympic* and *Titanic* were almost identical in size, *Titanic* was actually 1,004 tons heavier than her sister ship.

The third ship, *Gigantic*, was later renamed *Britannic*.

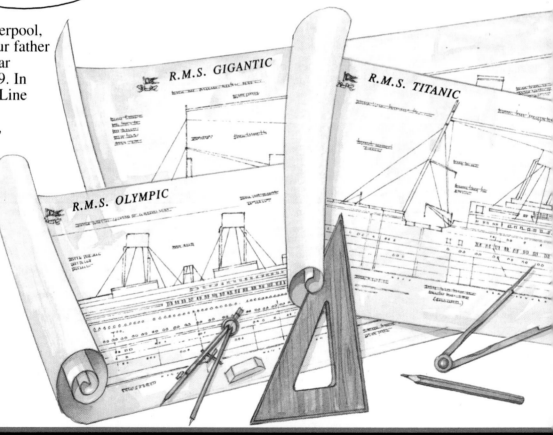

Titanic's Specifications

Ship weight: 46,329 gross registered tons (each ton is equal to 100 cubic ft)
Hull weight: 29,120 tons
Length: 882 ft 9 in (269 m)
Width: 92 ft 6 in (28 m)
Anchors: Three, with a total weight of 35 tons. Each chain link weighs about 175 lb.
Rudder weight: 20,250 lb
Boilers: 29, each weighing over 100 tons
Propellers: Three — one measuring 16 ft (5 m) across and two others, each measuring 23 ft (7 m) across
Funnels: Four, but only front three in use. Stern funnel used for ventilation.
Cost: Completed ship cost $7,500,000 in 1912. Today it would cost $400 million.

Handy Hint

You have designed one ship, so you might as well use the same design for two more.

How many passengers and crew on board?

Regulations state that the ship must carry lifeboats for 962 people. We have an extra four collapsible boats — room for 1,178 people.

We have room for 3,511 people.

Building the "Unsinkable" Ship

You have the plans, you have the dry dock, and now you need workers. The shipyard employs approximately 11,300 men to build *Titanic*. The central girders are first riveted to the keel to make the spine of the hull. Then 350 steel frames, with 10 levels of deck supports, form the skeleton of the ship. Bulkheads divide *Titanic's* hull into 16 compartments, which are said to be watertight because each extends well above the waterline. The ship could still float even if four of the compartments were filled with water! The shipyard is a dangerous place to work. Eight workers have been killed during construction, and over 240 accidents have been recorded by Harland and Wolff.

Aaah!

RIVETERS. They rivet steel plates, up to 6 ft (2 m) high and 36 ft (11 m) wide, weighing 5 tons, to the frames.

ANCHORS. *Titanic* needs three anchors. The heaviest weighs over 17 tons and will need a team of 20 horses to pull it from the foundry to the shipyard.

Launched but Not Completed

On May 31, 1911, *Titanic's* empty hull slides down the slipway. Sixty-two seconds later she enters the water for the first time. According to the custom of the shipyard and the White Star Line, the ship is launched unchristened.

Launch
OF
White Star Royal Mail
Triple-Screw Steamer
"TITANIC"
At Belfast,
Wednesday, 31st May, 1911, at 12.15 p.m.
Admit Bearer

Launch invitation

Who's Who?

Chief Engineer   Electrician   Boiler maker

Fireman   Stoker   Trimmer

Greaser   Apprentice

BOILER ROOMS. Seventy-three trimmers (who break up coal into small lumps) and 177 firemen work in the boiler rooms.

(speech) There are 29 boilers on this ship!

(speech) Yes, each 16.5 ft (5 m) high!

DOWN THE SLIPWAY. To get the massive ship down to the water, over 23 tons of soap, grease, and train oil are used. *Titanic* slides almost 1,800 ft before being brought to a halt by six anchor chains and two other piles of chains weighing 80 tons each.

Bloomin' backbreaking work for $27 a month.

All the machinery, including the engines, boilers, and funnels, is installed on board once the ship is afloat by using floating cranes. Once this is completed, the vessel can be towed away to a fitting-out berth. *Titanic's* interior will take 10 months and several million man-hours to complete. On April 2, 1912, the completed *Titanic* sets sail to begin its sea trials.

Captain and Crew

Captain Edward John Smith has been commodore of the White Star fleet since 1904. As he usually commands the White Star's newest ship, he will take charge of *Titanic* on her maiden voyage. Captain Smith is popular with his passengers and crew. Some wealthy passengers refuse to sail across the Atlantic unless he is captain. His salary is twice as much as Cunard captains', at $6,250 a year (that equals about $73,000 today), plus a no-collision bonus of $200! It will be Smith's last voyage, as he is retiring.

Members of the Crew:

CAPTAIN SMITH. He is in charge of 892 crew members, divided into three departments. The deck department is made up of 73 officers and seamen. The engine department has 325 crew, and the stewards department has 494.

Captain

OFFICERS. The officers are paid between $45 and $125 per month depending on length of service and experience.

Officer

SEAMEN. The able seamen are paid about $25 per month, depending on their duties. The deck crew works shifts of four hours on and eight hours off.

Seaman

If only we could get to New York in time to make the morning papers!

We don't want to force the engines when we are breaking them in, Mr. Ismay.

Handy Hint (for crew only)

Sluurpp

Be very nice to the passengers — tips can really boost your pay.

The Power of Steam

TRIPLE-SCREW STEAMER. *Titanic* is a triple-screw (three-propeller) steamer with five engines. Steam is produced in the six boiler rooms and piped to the engine rooms. Once the steam has passed through the engines, it is piped to the condensers, where it is cooled back into water and reused.

STEWARDS AND STEWARDESSES. Their duties and pay depend on which part of the ship they work in. Some wait on tables, others attend to cabins. One stewardess's monthly pay is about $17 for working 17 hours a day.

Stewardess and steward

Chef

CHEFS. There are two onboard chefs who supervise the two kitchens and a total of 35 cooks.

STOREKEEPERS. There are two storekeepers with two assistants on board.

Storekeeper

All Aboard

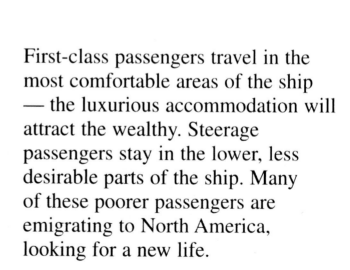

Manservant   Lady's maid   Nanny

Now the crew can welcome passengers aboard. There are three categories of passengers: first class, second class, and steerage (third class). You will travel in first class, naturally.

•R.M.S. TITANIC•
FIRST CLASS PASSAGE
TO NEW YORK
2 ADULTS
1 CHILD
3 SERVANTS
$750

•R.M.S. TITANIC•
SECOND CLASS PASSAGE
TO NEW YORK
2 ADULTS
1 CHILD
$145

First-class passengers travel in the most comfortable areas of the ship — the luxurious accommodation will attract the wealthy. Steerage passengers stay in the lower, less desirable parts of the ship. Many of these poorer passengers are emigrating to North America, looking for a new life.

STEERAGE. The accommodation in the steerage section of the ship is basic compared to other sections of the liner. Single men and women in steerage are separated by the entire length of the ship — men in the bow, women in the stern. Families are housed together in cabins.

•R.M.S. TITANIC•
THIRD CLASS PASSAGE
TO NEW YORK
2 ADULTS
2 CHILDREN
$120

Handy Hint

(for millionaires only)

Try to reserve a parlor suite with a 50-ft (15-m)-long private promenade deck. Book early to avoid disappointment — there are only two, and they cost $4,350 each (this would be about $70,000 today!).

Other Travelers

There will be plenty of dogs on *Titanic*, so an informal dog show is being planned for Monday, April 15.

Stocking the Ship
What You Will Need for a Transatlantic Crossing:

Titanic's food stores and equipment included 11,000 lb fresh fish, 4,000 lb dried fish, 7,500 lb bacon and ham, 25,000 lb poultry and game, 2,500 lb sausages, 1,500 gallons of fresh milk, 44,000 pieces of cutlery, 29,000 items of glassware, 75,000 lb fresh meat, 40,000 fresh eggs, 40 tons of potatoes, 800 bundles of asparagus, 1,000 bottles of wine, 15,000 bottles of ale and stout, 12,000 dinner plates, 1,000 oyster forks, 15,000 champagne glasses, 40,000 towels, 45,000 table napkins, 5 grand pianos, 14 wooden lifeboats, 2 wood cutters, 4 Englehardt collapsible boats, total lifeboat capacity 1,178 (Hold on, there are 2,206 passengers and crew! Never mind, the ship is "unsinkable" after all...), 3,560 life jackets, 49 life buoys.

Cargo list: Wakem & McLaughlin – 1 case wine, 25 case biscuits, 42 case wines. Spaulding & Brothers —34 case athletic goods. Park & Tilford—1 case toothpaste, 5 case drug sundries, 1 case brushware. Maltus & Ware—8 case orchids. Spencerian Pen Co.—4 case pens. Sherman Sons & Co.—7 case cotton. Claflin, H.B. & Co.—12 case cotton lace. Muser Brothers—3 case tissues. Isler & Guve—4 bales straw. Rydeman & Lassner—1 case Tulle (veil and scarf netting). Petry, P.H. & Co.—1 case Tulle. Metzger, A.S.—2 case Tulle. Mills & Gibb—20 case cottons, 1 case gloves. Field, Marshall & Co.—1 case gloves. NY Motion Pic. Co.—1 case film. Thorburn, J.M. & Co.— 3 case bulbs. Rawstick Trading Co.—28 bags sticks. Dujardin & Ladnick—10 box melons. Tiffany & Co.—1 cask china. Lustig Bros.—4 case straw hats. Kuyper, P.C. & Co.—1 case elastic cords, 1 case leather. Cohen, M. Bros.—5 package skins. Gross, Engle Co.—61 case Tulle. Gallia Textile Co.— 1 case lace goods. Calhoun, Robbins & Co.—1 case cotton laces, 1/2 case brushware. Victor & Achiles—1 case brushware. Baumgarten, Wm & Co.—3 case furniture. Spielman Co.—3 case silk crepe. Nottingham Lace Works— 2 case cotton. Naday & Fleisher—1 case laces. Rosenthal, Leo J. & Co.—4 case cotton. Leeming, T. & Co.—7 case biscuits. Crown Perfume Co.—3 case soap perfume. Meadows, T. & Co.—5 case books, 3 box samples, 1 case parchment. Thomas & Pierson—2 case hardware, 2 case books, 2 case furniture. American Express Co.—1 case elastics, 1 case Edison gramophones, 4 case hosiery...

he ship's full name is R.M.S. *Titanic* — the R.M.S. stands for Royal Mail Ship, as she will be used for shipping mail between Britain and the United States. There is a rumor that gold bars are also on board — but gold is transported and recorded as "mail" to keep it secret. *Titanic's* huge hold is filled with all sorts of things, from walnuts to ostrich feathers. Some of the wealthy passengers are even taking cars with them.

Five grand pianos?!

Don't worry, we'll squeeze 'em all in.

Handy Hint

Make sure all your items are insured. The total worth of the cargo on board *Titanic* in 1912 is $420,000, or about $6.7 million today.

Watch Out! Leaving Southampton

Rich and Famous On Board

At 12:00 on April 10, 1912, *Titanic* sets off from Southampton. Swift action by Captain Smith avoids a collision with another ship docked there, the *New York*. *Titanic* reaches Cherbourg, France, at dusk, where the wealthiest of the passengers embark. On April 11, *Titanic* arrives in Queenstown, Ireland, before setting off across the Atlantic.

John Jacob Astor VI

Benjamin Guggenheim

Mr. & Mrs. Isidor Straus

Colonel Archibald Gracie

MONEY, MONEY, MONEY. Among the first-class passengers is John Jacob Astor VI, the richest man on board. Benjamin Guggenheim's family made a fortune from mining, and Isidor Straus is the founder of Macy's department store in New York. Colonel Gracie's account of *Titanic's* maiden voyage makes him famous one day.

Route to New York

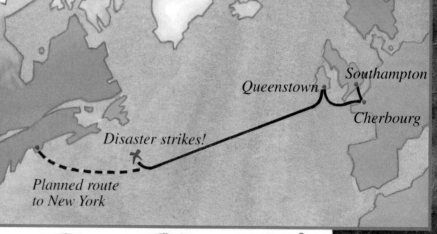

Southampton

Queenstown

Cherbourg

Disaster strikes!

Planned route to New York

18

Handy Hint

Ignore the 1898 book *Futility*. It tells the tale of a ship sinking on its maiden voyage with many lives lost due to too few lifeboats.

Oooh!

The wash from *Titanic's* huge propellers causes the *New York* to break her moorings and pulls her straight into the path of the *Titanic* (below).

Aaaargh!

A Tour of the Ship

FIRST-CLASS STATEROOMS. Working fireplaces are just one of the features in these lavishly decorated rooms. The rooms can accommodate one, two, or three people.

Your designers and shipbuilders have done a wonderful job, especially with the first-class sections. The dining rooms are elegant and spacious, and there are luxurious staterooms, cafés, and libraries. The main forward staircase is one of the ship's most dramatic features, lit from above by natural

First Class

STEERAGE. Third-class passengers stay in four-berth cabins. These are rather comfortable and would be used in second class on other ships.

light through a huge domed skylight. *Titanic* has three elevators in the first-class section and is the first ship to have one for second-class passengers. She is also the first ocean liner to have a swimming pool and a gym. Although second-class cabins are bigger and more luxurious than those in steerage, they look small and bare compared to the sumptuous rooms on the higher decks.

Handy Hint

Wheeze!

Try out the exercise machines in the gymnasium in first class. Passengers traveling in second class are allowed to look around first class before the ship sets sail.

Second Class

Steerage (Third Class)

Icebergs Ahead...

Captain's Log: April 14, 1912

...the engines have never run so fast...

Captain Smith is a guest of Mr. and Mrs. Widener at dinner in the restaurant on B deck.

Another warning, Captain.

He receives another message about icebergs — the sixth warning today.

The ship is now steaming toward New York at speeds of more than 22.5 knots (26 mph) — so fast that she will arrive a day early. Ice warnings are coming in from other ships in this area of the North Atlantic. The lookout crew in the crow's nest have been warned to watch out for icebergs — but their binoculars were left behind in Southampton! At 11:40 P.M., you are awoken by strange scraping noises. Putting a coat on over your pyjamas, you head for the ship's bridge. Captain Smith tells you the ship has struck ice and is seriously damaged, but you don't believe him.

It's very cold, Officer Lightoller.

One degree above freezing, Sir.

It is a moonless evening, and the sea is calm. Captain Smith leaves the bridge to go to bed at 9:20 P.M.

When the watch changes at 10:00 P.M., Officer Murdoch takes charge of the wheel on the bridge.

11:40 P.M. Lookouts spot an iceberg. The ship's engines are put into reverse, but it is too late, and *Titanic* scrapes along the side.

Crrrunch!

Handy Hint

Send emergency messages by Morse code. Use the traditional distress signal, CQD, and try the new one, SOS, because it is quicker and easier to send.

DAMAGE TO THE SHIP. Hitting the iceberg made the hull plates buckle. The water pressure on the weakened joints makes the rivets pop out, and the plates are pushed apart.

We've struck an iceberg, sir!

11:50 P.M. Captain Smith returns to the bridge and orders the watertight doors closed. This will make the ship unsinkable.

12:00 A.M. You both inspect the ship. Water is gushing into the hull, flowing above the bulkheads and pulling the ship down.

Captain Smith faces the grim reality that his ship is sinking. The telegraph operator begins sending emergency messages.

23

Wake Up! Life Jackets On!

What Do You Do?

PANIC?!

Stay calm...

...or stay in bed?!

Soon after midnight, Captain Smith orders the lifeboats prepared, and adds that women and children should evacuate *Titanic* before the men. The first lifeboat, number seven, splashes into the water at 12:25 A.M., 45 minutes after the collision. It contains 28 passengers, but has space for 65. By 1:20 A.M., six lifeboats have left the ship. Deep in the boiler and engine rooms, engineers and crew risk their own safety to keep the lights burning and the pumps working. You help people into the lifeboats, then quietly slip yourself into collapsible boat C.

COME BACK! Using a megaphone, Captain Smith orders several of the half-empty lifeboats to return to the ship to pick up more passengers. None respond because they are afraid of becoming overloaded.

SINKING? I DON'T BELIEVE IT.
Few passengers believe that the ship is really sinking. The thought of descending into the darkness of the icy Atlantic makes many people stay on deck in the hope of being rescued. A lot of the female passengers refuse to be separated from their husbands.

Sinking Fast

How Titanic Sinks:

BULKHEADS. Six compartments are split open, and even the watertight doors canot save the ship.

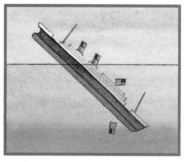

FRONT FIRST. The weight of the water in the front compartments pulls the bow of the ship downward.

BOW SUBMERGED. The ship tears apart, and the bow heads for the ocean floor.

FINAL MINUTES. The stern bobs upright for five minutes before filling with water and sinking.

By 2:15 A.M. on April 15, fourteen lifeboats, two emergency boats, and four collapsibles have left the ship. Over 1,500 people remain on board. *Titanic's* stern begins to rise up out of the ocean. Water is pouring in through the open portholes. The ship's lights are still on, and the band bravely continues to play on deck. At 2:18 A.M., the lights start to flicker off and on. Rivets begin to pop, and deck planks snap as the ship begins to break in two. The noise is deafening. Once the bow is totally submerged, it finally rips apart from the rest of the ship and plunges to the ocean floor. Just a few minutes later, you turn your back as *Titanic's* stern slides under the water. Captain Smith is last seen on the bridge, having given final orders to abandon ship.

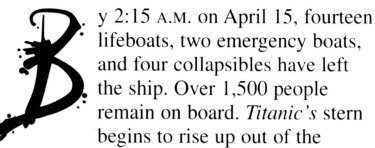

Handy Hint

Help the crew of your lifeboat row away from the ship so you aren't sucked down with her when she sinks.

Molly Brown

Mrs. Margaret Brown becomes known as the "Unsinkable Molly Brown" for taking command of lifeboat number 6 and demanding that women be allowed to row as well as men.

TITANIC

The Aftermath

Only one person is rescued alive from the freezing sea. Over 1,500 lives are lost, but only 306 of those bodies are picked up. The dead from first class are embalmed and taken home for burial, but those from third class and crew members are sewn up in heavy linen and buried at sea. The wages of the 214 surviving crew are calculated and paid up to the moment the ship sank.

At the official inquiries that follow, many questions are asked: Should *Titanic* have been sailing more slowly? Should she have carried more lifeboats? After the disaster, a change in the law ensures that all passenger ships carry enough lifeboats for everyone on board and that regular lifeboat drills be held. All ships also have to have 24-hour radio watch.

They are frozen to death, not drowned.

There's someone alive!

S.S. Carpathia to the Rescue

S.S. CARPATHIA. This Cunard ship is 58 miles (93 km) away from *Titanic* when she receives the SOS signal. She steams to the scene of the disaster and arrives at 4:10 A.M.

SURVIVORS TAKEN TO NEW YORK. *Carpathia* cruises the area looking for any last survivors before setting sail for New York with 705 of *Titanic's* stunned passengers on board.

What Happens to You?

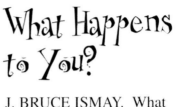

J. BRUCE ISMAY. What has happened to J. Bruce Ismay, the man who dreamed of building the greatest liners in the world? You have survived the disaster, but your reputation is ruined. Within a year you resign from the White Star Line and donate $50,000 to the pensions fund for widows of *Titanic* crew. You die in 1937 at the age of 74, having never made any further public statement about *Titanic* since the inquiries into the disaster.

Glossary

Berth A fixed bunk on a ship for sleeping in, or a ship's place in dock.

Bow The front end of a boat or ship.

Bridge The place on a ship where the captain and officers control every other part of the ship.

Bulkhead An upright partition separating the compartments of a ship.

Collapsible boat A type of lifeboat that is folded up and stored until needed.

Commodore The senior captain of a shipping line.

CQD The standard ship distress call, first used in 1903. "CQ" was the signal for listening radio operators to stop and pay attention; adding the "D" meant distress.

Crow's nest A shelter or platform high up the mast of a ship for a lookout person.

Dry dock An area for building or repairing ships, from which water can be pumped out.

Emigrant A person who leaves his or her own country to go and live in another.

Hull The body or frame of a ship.

Keel The "backbone" of a ship along which the rest of the hull is built up.

Mooring A fixed object that a ship can be tied to.

Morse code A set of dots, dashes, and spaces used to send messages via radio to other ships or to land.

Porthole A window in the side of a ship.

Rivet A metal device for holding sheets of metal together.

SOS The Morse code distress signal that came into official use in 1908. The three dots, three dashes, and three dots are quick and easy to recognize and send.

Steerage The part of a ship with accommodation for passengers with the cheapest tickets, or third class.

Stern The back end of a boat or ship.

Transatlantic Spanning across the Atlantic Ocean.

Ventilation The forced movement of air around a room or rooms.

Waterline The line along which the surface of water touches the side of a ship.

Index